SCOTTISH TERRIERS

by Susan H. Gray

Published in the United States of America by The Child's World®
1980 Lookout Drive • Mankato, MN 56003-1705
800-599-READ • www.childsworld.com

PHOTO CREDITS
© Daniel Dempster Photography/Alamy: 29
© David McGill/Alamy: 25
© Digital Archive Japan/Alamy: cover, 1
© imagebroker/Alamy: 17
© iStockphoto.com/Neeley Spotts: 15
© iStockphoto.com/Robyn Glover: 21
© Jeanne White/Photo Researchers, Inc.: 13
© Malcolm Freeman/Alamy: 27
© Mark Raycroft/Minden Pictures: 23
© Petra Wegner/Alamy: 9
© PhotoStockFile/Alamy: 11
© Wendy Conway/Alamy: 19

ACKNOWLEDGMENTS
The Child's World®: Mary Berendes, Publishing Director;
Katherine Stevenson, Editor

The Design Lab: Kathleen Petelinsek, Design and Page Production

LIBRARY OF CONGRESS CATALOGING-IN-PUBLICATION DATA
Gray, Susan Heinrichs.
  Scottish terriers / by Susan H. Gray.
     p. cm.—(Domestic dogs)
  ISBN-13: 978-1-59296-968-5 (library bound: alk. paper)
  1. Scottish terrier—Juvenile literature. I. Title.
  SF429.S4G67 2008
  636.755—dc22   2007020795

Table of Contents

NAME That DOG!

What dog has bushy eyebrows and a beard? What dog is named after a country in Great Britain? What dog gets its hair gently pulled out by hand? What dog has been owned by American presidents? If you said the Scottish terrier, you are correct!

5

Hard-Working Farm Dogs

Years ago, many farmers in Great Britain had dogs. The dogs helped keep crops and farm animals safe. Foxes, badgers, weasels, and rats could be big pests. The dogs would chase these animals away. Some dogs chased the animals right into their burrows and dens. They even dug up the burrows. These dogs were known as *terriers*.

Great Britain is an island in Europe. It includes England, Scotland, and Wales. The map below shows where Great Britain is on Earth. The map on the right shows a closer view.

Atlantic Ocean

Scotland

North Sea

Northern Ireland

Ireland

England

Great Britain

Wales

Atlantic Ocean

English Channel

France

7

Scottish terriers have long bodies that are low to the ground. These dogs can crawl into some animals' burrows.

People in Great Britain liked different kinds of terriers. Some liked short-haired terriers. Others liked long-haired terriers better. Some liked smaller terriers. And others liked bigger, stronger dogs.

Many people in Scotland liked small terriers that had wiry hair. These dogs became known as Scottish terriers.

In 1883, a dog lover brought Scottish terriers to the United States. Soon "Scotties" began appearing in dog shows. Many Americans learned about the little terriers. The dogs became very **popular** pets! Other dog **breeds** are now more common in America. But people still love little Scotties.

Scottish terriers were once called Aberdeen terriers. Aberdeen is a city in Scotland.

Scotties are very watchful dogs. They are curious about many things.

Tough Little Terriers

Scottish terriers are small and strong. Their legs are short. Adults are only about 10 inches (25 centimeters) tall at the shoulders. They weigh about 20 pounds (9 kilograms). Scottish terriers are very strong for their size. Their legs are powerful. That helps these dogs be good diggers!

A Scottie's head looks too long for its body. The small, pointy ears stand straight up. The eyes are dark, and the nose is black.

This Scottie is enjoying a summer day.

Scotland often has cold, wet weather. Scottish terriers' fur is made for such weather. The fur close to their bodies is thick and soft. It keeps the dogs warm. Their outer fur is different. The hairs are long, hard, and wiry. This outer coat sheds water easily.

Many Scotties are gray or black. Others are called "wheaten." They are the color of straw, or almost white. Others have coats with streaks or splotches. They are called "brindle."

Owners often clip the hair on Scotties' faces. That gives the dogs beards and bushy eyebrows.

Scottish terriers have big teeth for such little dogs. Some owners brush their dogs' teeth to keep them clean and bright.

This Scottie has a wheaten-colored coat.

13

Minds of Their Own?

Scottie owners often say these dogs have minds of their own. That is because Scotties can be hard to train. They are certainly smart enough to learn **commands**. But they like to work on their own. Years ago, they were raised to chase animals. They got used to their freedom. They got used to thinking for themselves. They might not see any reason to **obey** commands. Owners must be **patient** when training them.

Some Scotties like to rest instead of obeying their owners.

15

Scottish terriers are very **loyal**. They love to be with their owners. They are happiest when they are with people they know. In fact, they bark loudly at visitors. They might not welcome strangers into their homes.

Scotties make great pets for people in small houses or apartments. They can get enough exercise indoors. These dogs are good pets for adults and older children. Small children often make noises that upset them.

People have given the Scottish terrier a nickname—the Diehard.

Owners often give these dogs Scottish names, such as MacDougal, Kirk, Angus, or Campbell.

This Scottie is its owner's best friend.

Scottie Puppies

Most Scottish terrier mothers have four or five puppies in a **litter**. The furry newborns have soft ears, round heads, and short tails. For the first two weeks, they are helpless. Their eyes are closed, and they cannot see. Their ears cannot hear. They spend all of their time with their mother. She gives them food, safety, and warmth. After three weeks, things have changed! The pups can see, hear, and move around.

Like all puppies, newborn Scotties drink their mother's milk.

This is an important time in the puppies' lives. The pups need to be kept from any danger. Even loud noises can upset them. The puppies should still be with their mothers. They need to feel safe at this age. If they do not, they might be nervous or shy as adults. They might be harder to train.

Like other puppies, Scottish terriers grow quickly. After four months, they weigh half as much as adults.

The puppies keep growing. They get a little braver. They get interested in the world around them. The brothers and sisters spend a lot of time playing. That teaches them to get along with other animals. They learn to get along with people, too. Finally they are ready to go to their new homes.

This Scottie puppy is just a few weeks old. He has found a toy to play with!

21

Pets and Friends

The Scottish terrier's main job is to be a good pet. Many owners just enjoy these dogs as friends. Some owners also enter Scotties in **contests**. In obedience contests, the dogs show how well they obey commands. In other contests, they show how well they can follow smells.

Scotties often take part in **agility** contests. The dogs must run through tunnels. They must jump through tires and leap over fences. And they must move fast! Even though Scotties are small, they often do well in agility contests.

This Scottie is running through a tunnel in an agility contest.

In dog shows, people look at the dogs carefully. They look at how good-looking the dogs are. They watch how well the dogs behave. They look closely at each Scottish terrier. They feel the dog's coat. They check its color. They make sure the coat is wiry. They make sure the dog has a dark nose and dark eyes. They watch how the dog holds its head and tail. It should hold them proudly! They make sure the dog's teeth meet correctly. They watch how the dog moves. The best dogs win awards.

Several American presidents have had Scotties as pets. President Franklin D. Roosevelt owned Fala. President Ronald Reagan owned two Scotties, Scotch and Soda. President George W. Bush owns Barney and Miss Beazley.

This Scottie is being shown in a dog show.

Caring for a Scottie

Scottish terriers are strong and smart. Like most dogs, they like to go outside and exercise. Scotties love to go for walks, too. But they must be kept on a leash. They want to chase other animals. Without a leash, they often run after squirrels or cats.

Some Scotties get a problem called Scottie Cramp. When they get too excited, they cannot move well. They might fall over. They might even roll over. They are not in

This Scottie's owner keeps his pet safe by keeping her on a leash.

27

pain. They are not in danger. They just need to settle down. Then they will be all right.

Scotties' coats need lots of care and **grooming**. They should be brushed often. That keeps the fur from getting tangled. The hair should also be clipped or *stripped*. Stripping thins the coats of wire-haired dogs. A groomer pulls out the dead, wiry hairs. They come out easily, without hurting the dog. The new hair that grows in will be wiry. If the dogs are clipped instead, their fur grows in soft.

Most Scotties live long, healthy lives. In fact, they can live well into their teens. That is a nice, long time to be their owners' friends!

Scottish terriers love to dig. If left outside, they might tear up a garden. Or they might burrow under a fence.

This Scottie is being groomed for a dog show.

29

Glossary

agility (uh-JIH-luh-tee) Agility is being able to move quickly and easily. Scottish terriers have great agility for their size.

breeds (BREEDZ) Breeds are certain types of an animal. Scottish terriers are a well-known dog breed.

commands (kuh-MANDZ) Commands are orders to do certain things. Scotties can learn to follow commands.

contests (KON-tests) Contests are meets where people or animals try to win by being the best. Owners sometimes enter Scotties in contests.

grooming (GROOM-ing) Grooming an animal is cleaning and brushing it. Scotties need grooming.

litter (LIH-tur) A litter is a group of babies born to one animal. Scotties' litters often have four or five puppies.

loyal (LOY-ul) To be loyal is to be true to something and stand up for it. Scotties are loyal to their owners.

obey (oh-BAY) To obey someone is to do what the person says. Scotties do not always want to obey their owners.

patient (PAY-shunt) Being patient means facing problems without getting upset. Owners need to be patient when training Scotties.

popular (PAH-pyuh-lur) When something is popular, it is liked by lots of people. Scotties are popular.

To Find Out More

Books to Read

American Kennel Club. *The Complete Dog Book for Kids.* New York: Howell Book House, 1996.

Lee, Muriel P. *Scottish Terrier.* Allenhurst, NJ: Kennel Club Books, 2004.

Vanderlip, Sharon. *Scottish Terriers.* Hauppauge, NY: Barron's Educational Series, 2001.

Weigand, Edith S. *Scottie-Robbie: The Story of a True Champion.* Denver, CO: Zhera Publications, 2000.

Places to Contact

American Kennel Club (AKC) Headquarters
260 Madison Ave, New York, NY 10016
Telephone: 212-696-8200

On the Web

Visit our Web site for lots of links about Scottish terriers:

http://www.childsworld.com/links

Note to Parents, Teachers, and Librarians: We routinely check our Web links to make sure they're safe, active sites—so encourage your readers to check them out!

Index

About the Author

Susan H. Gray has a Master's degree in zoology. She has written more than 70 science and reference books for children. She loves to garden and play the piano. Susan lives in Cabot, Arkansas, with her husband Michael and many pets.